Sacred Solos
Primer Level

Supplement to All Piano and Keyboard Methods

Compiled, Arranged, and Edited by Wesley Schaum

Foreword

This series of sacred solos includes favorite hymns, gospel songs, spirituals and sacred music from the classical repertoire. The selections have been made to appeal to students of all ages and also with regard to popularity in many different churches. Some of the hymn tunes may be known with different titles and lyrics.

Duet accompaniments offer many possibilities for recitals and Sunday school participation. The duets help provide valuable rhythmic training and ensemble experience. Duets are recommended for use at home as well as at the lesson. The person playing the accompaniment is free to add pedal according to his/her own taste.

Contents

All Hail the Power of Jesus' Name 11

Amazing Grace 23

Come Thou Almighty King 17

Fairest Lord Jesus 7

Faith of Our Fathers 4

For the Beauty of the Earth 15

Holy, Holy, Holy 19

Jesu, Joy of Man's Desiring 9

Jesus Loves Me, This I Know 3

Stand Up for Jesus 21

When the Saints Go Marching In 13

To access audio visit:
www.halleonard.com/mylibrary

Enter Code
4569-2571-9803-6884

ISBN 978-1-4950-8214-6

EXCLUSIVELY DISTRIBUTED BY

Visit Hal Leonard Online at
www.halleonard.com

Contact Us:
Hal Leonard
7777 West Bluemound Road
Milwaukee, WI 53213
Email: info@halleonard.com

In Europe contact:
Hal Leonard Europe Limited
Distribution Centre, Newmarket Road
Bury St Edmunds, Suffolk, IP33 3YB
Email: info@halleonardeurope.com

In Australia contact:
Hal Leonard Australia Pty. Ltd.
4 Lentara Court
Cheltenham, Victoria, 3192 Australia
Email: info@halleonard.com.au

Duet Accompaniment

Notes with **stems up** are to be played with the **right** hand. Notes with **stems down** are to be played with the **left** hand.

Jesus Loves Me, This I Know

Anna Warner

William B. Bradbury

Semplice

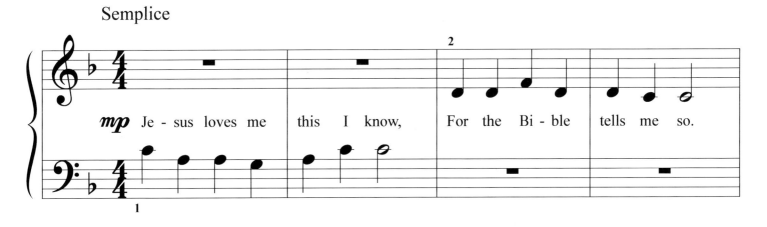

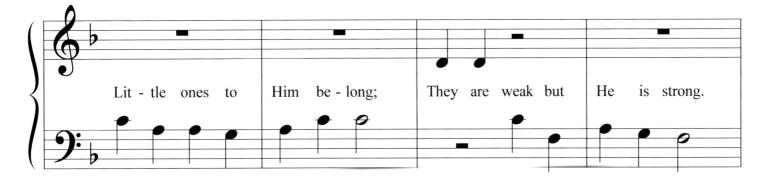

Faith of Our Fathers

Frederick W. Faber

Henry F. Hemy

Moderato

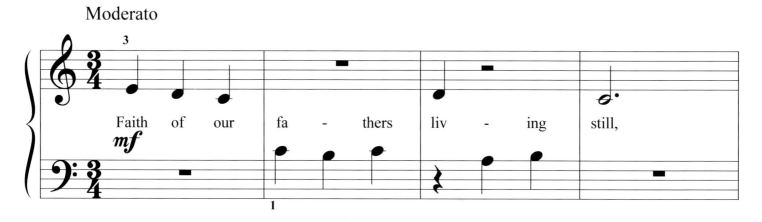

Faith of our fa - thers liv - ing still,

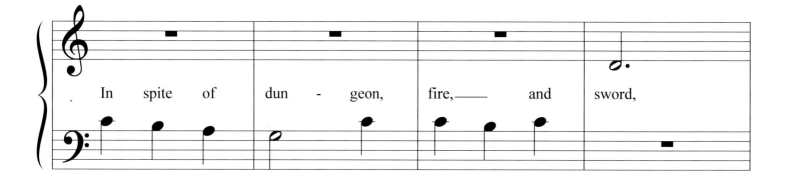

In spite of dun - geon, fire,—— and sword,

Duet Accompaniment

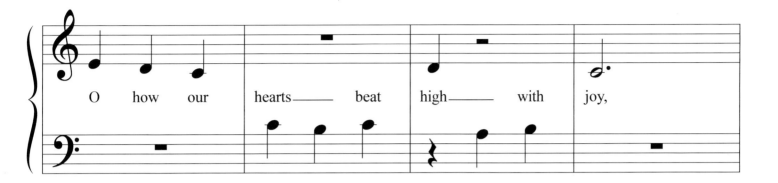

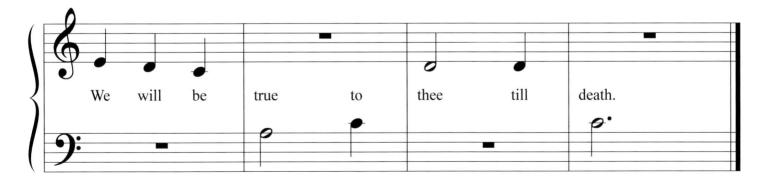

Duet Accompaniment

Fairest Lord Jesus

Richard S. Willis

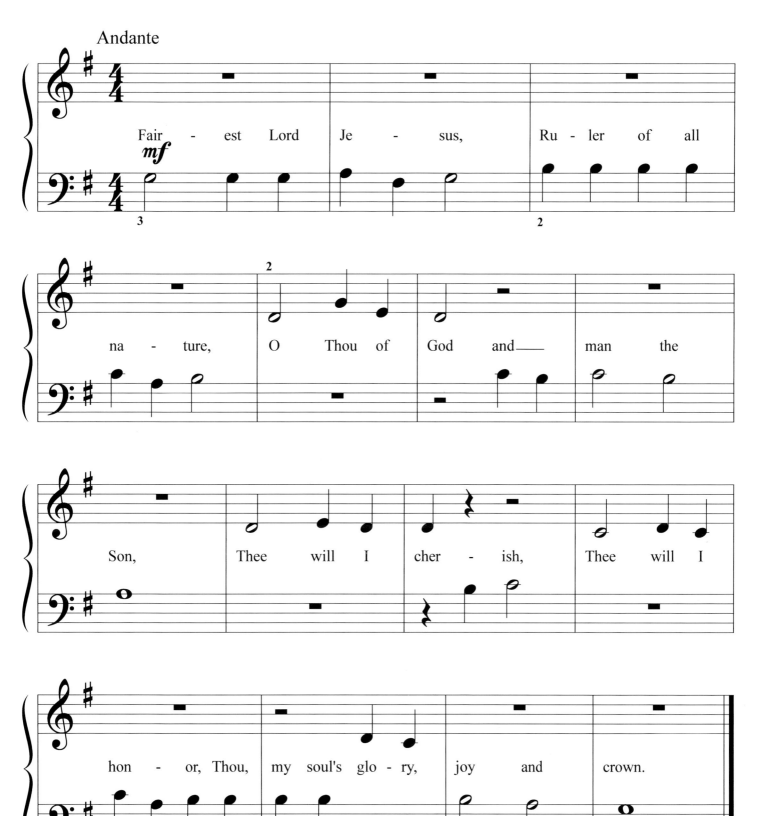

Duet Accompaniment

Jesu, Joy of Man's Desiring

J.S. Bach

Andante

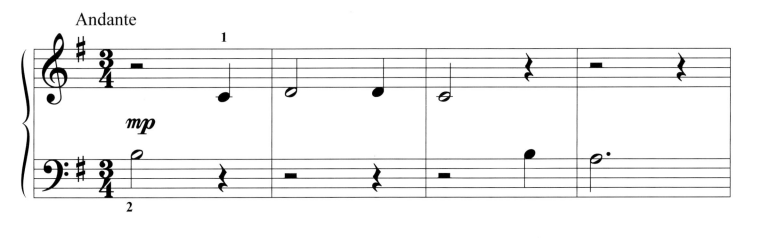

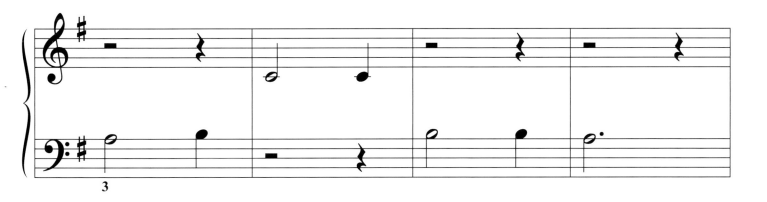

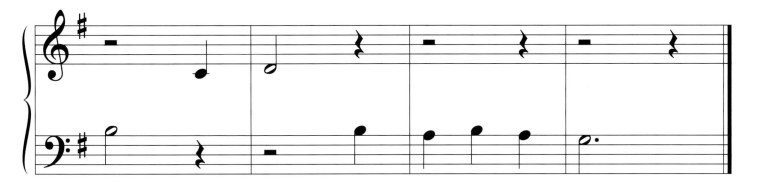

Duet Accompaniment

All Hail the Power of Jesus' Name

Edward Perronet

Oliver Holden

Moderato

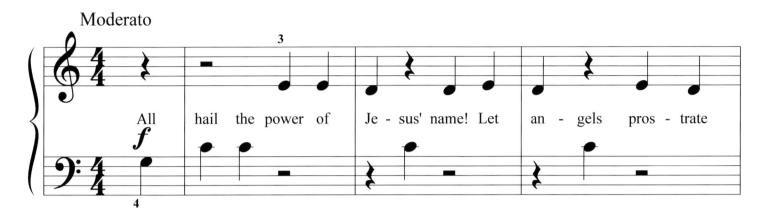

All hail the power of Je - sus' name! Let an - gels pros - trate

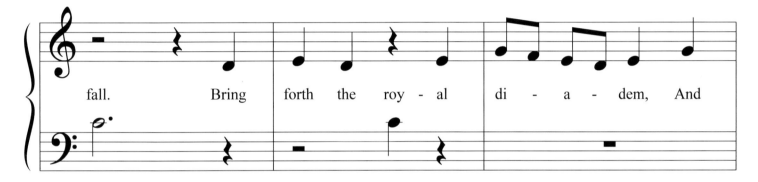

fall. Bring forth the roy - al di - a - dem, And

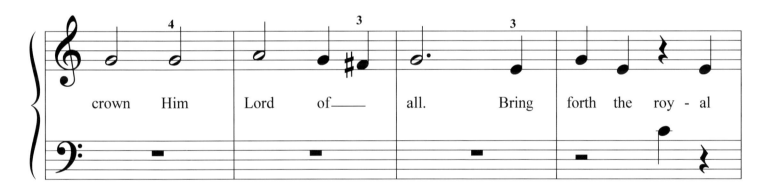

crown Him Lord of—— all. Bring forth the roy - al

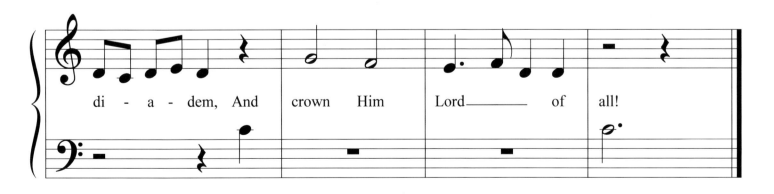

di - a - dem, And crown Him Lord—— of all!

Duet Accompaniment

When the Saints Go Marching In

American Folk Song

Allegro

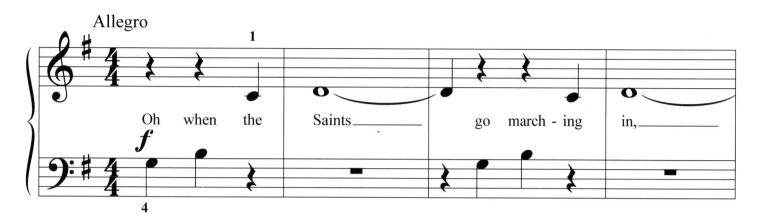

Oh when the Saints_____ go march - ing in,_____

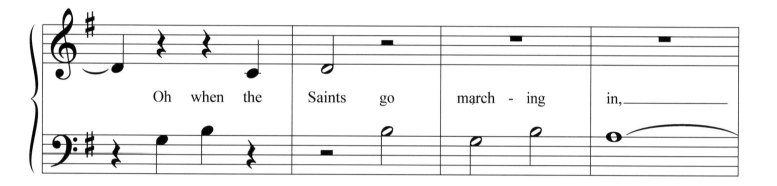

Oh when the Saints go march - ing in,_____

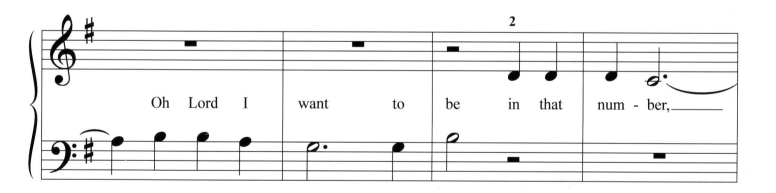

Oh Lord I want to be in that num - ber,_____

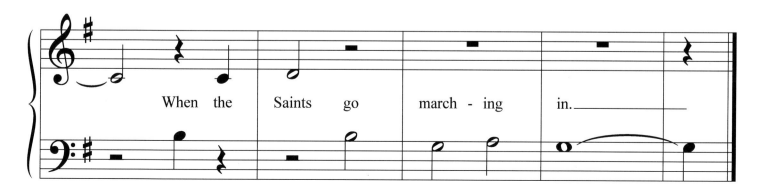

When the Saints go march - ing in._____

Duet Accompaniment

For the Beauty of the Earth

Folliott S. Pierpoint

Conrad Kocher

Andante

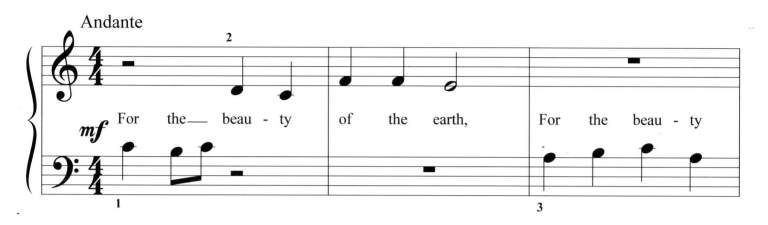

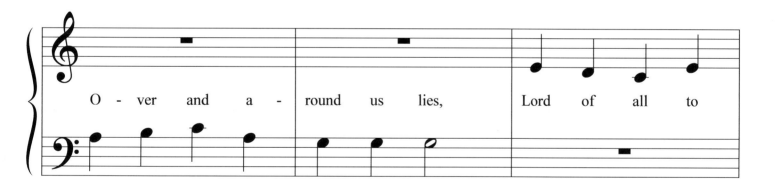

Duet Accompaniment

Come Thou Almighty King

Author Unknown

Felice Giardini

Maestoso

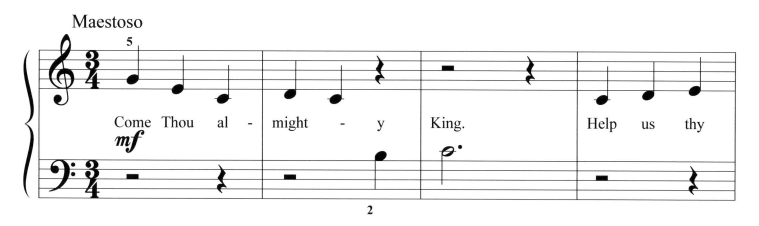

Come Thou al - might - y King. Help us thy

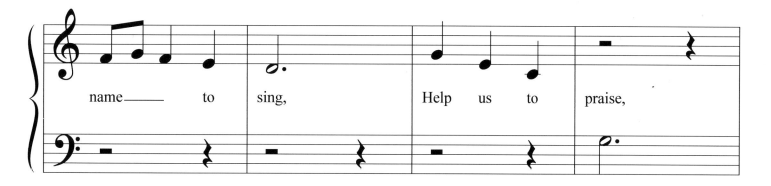

name——— to sing, Help us to praise,

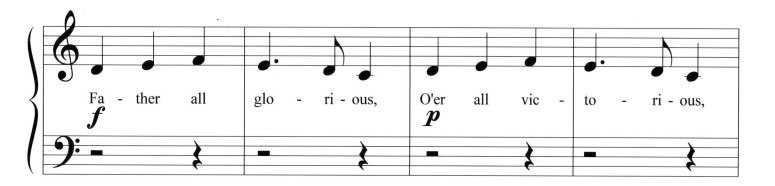

Fa - ther all glo - ri - ous, O'er all vic - to - ri - ous,

Come and reign o - ver us, An - cient of Days!

Duet Accompaniment

Holy, Holy, Holy

Reginald Heber

Rev. John B. Dykes

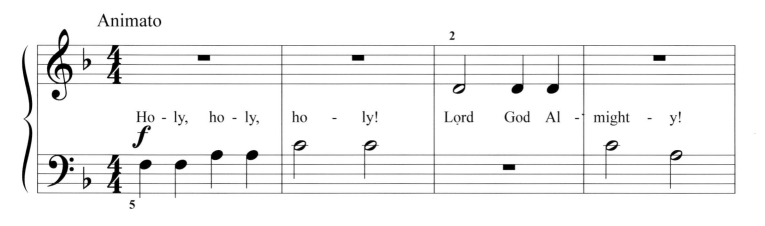

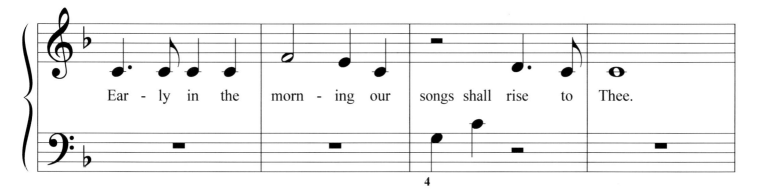

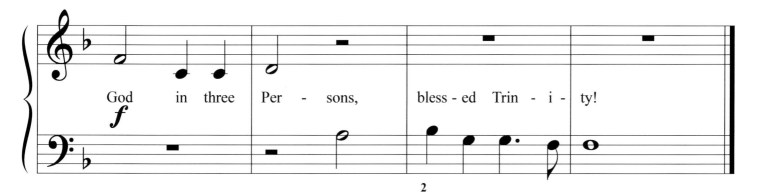

Duet Accompaniment

Stand Up for Jesus

George Duffield

George J. Webb

Allegretto

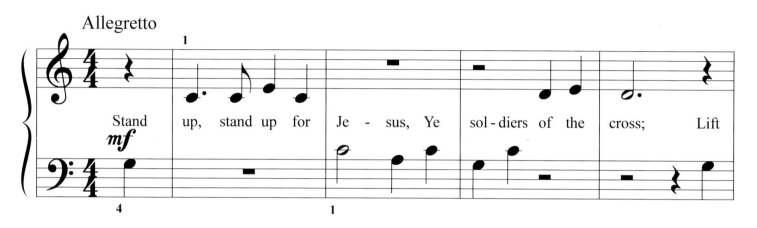

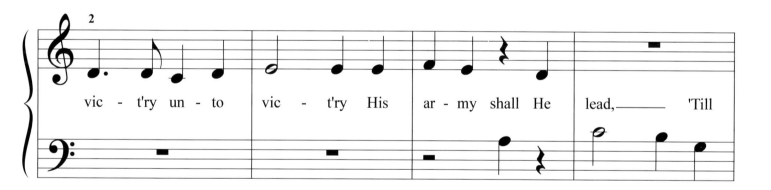

Duet Accompaniment

Amazing Grace

John Newton

Early American Melody

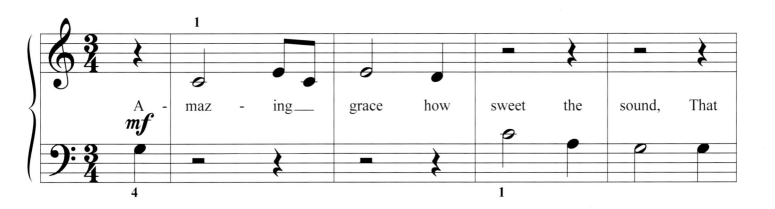

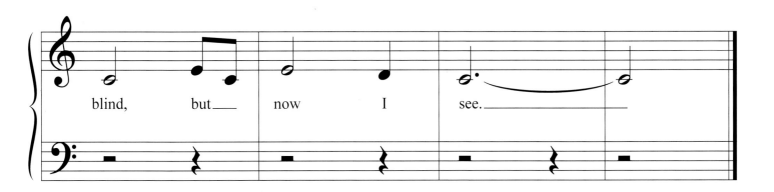

MORE GREAT SCHAUM PUBLICATIONS

FINGERPOWER®

by John W. Schaum
Physical training and discipline
are needed for both athletics and
keyboard playing. Keyboard muscle
conditioning is called technique.
technique exercises are as important
to the keyboard player as workouts
and calisthenics are to the athlete.
Schaum's *Fingerpower* books
are dedicated to development
of individual finger strength and
dexterity in both hands.

00645334	Primer Level – Book Only	$7.99
00645016	Primer Level – Book/Audio	$9.99
00645335	Level 1 – Book Only	$6.99
00645019	Level 1 – Book/Audio	$8.99
00645336	Level 2 – Book Only	$7.99
00645022	Level 2 – Book/Audio	$9.99
00645337	Level 3 – Book Only	$6.99
00645025	Level 3 – Book/Audio	$7.99
00645338	Level 4 – Book Only	$6.99
00645028	Level 4 – Book/Audio	$9.99
00645339	Level 5 Book Only	$7.99
00645340	Level 6 Book Only	$7.99

FINGERPOWER® ETUDES

Melodic exercises crafted by master
technique composers. Modified or
transposed etudes provide equal
hand development with a planned
variety of technical styles, keys, and
time signatures.

00645392	Primer Level	$6.99
00645393	Level 1	$6.99
00645394	Level 2	$6.99
00645395	Level 3	$6.99
00645396	Level 4	$6.99

FINGERPOWER® FUN

arr. Wesley Schaum
Early Elementary Level
Musical experiences beyond the
traditional *Fingerpower* books that
include fun-to-play pieces with finger
exercises and duet accompaniments.
Short technique preparatory drills
(finger workouts) focus on melodic
patterns found in each piece.

00645126	Primer Level	$6.95
00645127	Level 1	$6.99
00645128	Level 2	$6.95
00645129	Level 3	$6.99
00645144	Level 4	$6.95

FINGERPOWER® POP

arr. by James Poteat
10 great pop piano solo
arrangements with fun technical
warm-ups that complement the
Fingerpower series! Can also be
used as motivating supplements
to any method and in any learning
situation.

00237508	Primer Level	$9.99
00237510	Level 1	$9.99
00282865	Level 2	$9.99
00282866	Level 3	$9.99
00282867	Level 4	$10.99

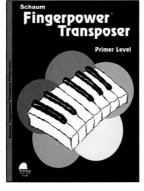

FINGERPOWER® TRANSPOSER

by Wesley Schaum
Early Elementary Level
This book includes 21 short,
8-measure exercises using 5-finger
patterns. Positions are based on C,F,
and G major and no key signatures
are used. Patterns involve intervals
of 3rds, 4ths, and 5ths up and down
and are transposed from C to F and
F to C, C to G and G to C, G to F and
F to G.

00645150	Primer Level	$6.95
00645151	Level 1	$6.95
00645152	Level 2	$6.95
00645154	Level 3	$6.95
00645156	Level 4	$6.99

JUMBO STAFF MANUSCRIPT BOOK

This pad features 24 pages with 4
staves per page.
00645936 . . . . $4.25

CERTIFICATE OF MUSICAL ACHIEVEMENT

Reward your students for their hard
work with these official 8x10-inch
certificates that you can customize.
12 per package.
00645938 . . . . $6.99

SCHAUM LESSON ASSIGNMENT BOOK

by John Schaum
With space for 32 weeks, this book
will help keep students on the right
track for their practice time.
00645935 . . . . $3.95

HAL•LEONARD®
www.halleonard.com

0322

Prices, contents, and availability subject to change without notice.

355